MEDITATIONS
of the
MIND

DOROTHY CARTER

Copyright © 2021 by Dorothy Carter

All rights reserved. No part of this publication may be reproduced, distributed, or transmitted in any form or by any means, including photocopying, recording, or other electronic or mechanical methods, without the prior written permission of the publisher, except in the case brief quotations embodied in critical reviews and other noncommercial uses permitted by copyright law.

ISBN: 978-1-954341-87-6 (Paperback)

The views expressed in this book are solely those of the author and do not necessarily reflect the views of the publisher, and the publisher hereby disclaims any responsibility for them.

Writers' Branding
1800-608-6550
www.writersbranding.com
orders@writersbranding.com

Introduction

Meditations of the Mind is a collection of poems designed for the edification of an all powerful God, who is greater than anything in Heaven, or on Earth. I pray that whoever reads these words will find hope where they thought there was none. I ask you to let these poems resonate in your mind, and realize that God is always with us, no matter where we are.

Dedications

This book is dedicated to a God who deserves all praise. A God who gave me the words to put down on these pages. I could do nothing without him. To all my family members, past and present, who have given me the life experiences that I write about. To my church family, who has supported me in my writing, and called on me to read my poems in the worship service.

A special thanks to my sister, Mrs. Edna Hargraves, my friends, Mrs. Rose Hall, Mrs. Gloria Blankenship, and Mrs. Annie George for appreciating and encouraging my work and encouraging me also. Last but not least, a very special thanks to my granddaughter, Taylor Davis, for assisting me in typing this book. I would like to thank all the Xlibris family for their time and patience with me in guiding me through this process. All the love and support is highly appreciated and keeps me motivated to do what I love.

Foreword

I grew up in the state of Arkansas in a little town called Marianna. I am the 7th child of eleven children, mother of two, and grandmother of two. I have always loved poetry of any style. I have been writing poetry throughout my entire life. I started at the age of fifteen. It was hard for me to express my feelings outwardly, so I put them in words; happy, sad, or in awe of nature itself. All the people that surrounded me became a forum for my writing. What started as a hobby transformed into a gift when I became a Christian. God gave me the inspiration to start writing spiritual poetry to encourage someone in their faith journey, to uplift the broken hearted, and to instill hope to those who feel like giving up, so that they may invite Christ into their lives and gain salvation and peace of mind in this constantly changing society.

Seek To Find

I discover new meaning every time I read the word of God; sometimes the lessons learned can be very hard. Things you thought you really understood, opens up a new revelation designed for your good. If we seek for answers within God's word; we will find there's much more we haven't heard. As Christians, we think we know all there is to know, but as long as we seek, we will continually grow. No one person can discern it all, but if we search the scriptures , God will answer our call.

Medication

Prayer is what gets me through, when I'm racked with pain and don't know what else to do. Doctors prescribe medicine for my health needs; but God is the power that cause them to succeed. I take the medication as I am told, then wait on God to take control.

Committed

Christians today are afraid to stand for God and be bold; God wants our commitment, and his truth to be told. We are his disciples, and we are to tell the unsaved about his plan of salvation, so their souls can be saved, and join his heavenly nation. How can we get the unsaved to come in; when we ourselves are committing sin. The unsaved expect more from us, or we won't gain their respect or trust. We need to get real, and take a major stand, against all that's wrong in our churches, brought in by man. Our commitment to God should be first and foremost; if we are striving to join him and his heavenly host.

Home On High

Streets of pearl and gates of gold, oh what a sight we will behold. The glory of God shining all around; when we make it in to get our crown. No more sickness, no more pain; eternal life we will have gained. We will sing in the heavenly choir, with one goal only; to praise God and never tire. No more arguing, no more fights, just praising God day and night. Oh what a wonderful time it will be, to join the one who set us free. Rejoice, and be thankful to God; for the perfect gift presented to us from the love in his heart.

Quick To Judge

We are all guilty of judging others at one time or another, but we don't know their situation or trouble. We look at the outer appearance, but God looks at the heart; we draw our own conclusion, but God knows from the start. If we just took the time, to get to know them we would find; they are completely different from what we thought in our mind.

Wayward People

Lord, we thank you for this day, and all our yesterdays; you have kept us in all our stubborn ways. When we are contrary to your will, you just keep on blessing us still. We are so ungrateful and don't recognize, we can't make it without you on our side. We are not worthy of your amazing love, but you keep on keeping us from above. By your mercy we have a chance, to live for you and obey your command...

I Must Write

When I have no words to write; God gives new inspiration to be brought to light, words that continually flow; filling my mind as I go. I begin writing as fast as I can; I do not stop until the words slow my hand. I can't stop writing until I get them all down; if I miss the opportunity it won't come back around. When God give me the words, they are there for a time; I can't recall them, because he put them in my mind. I wait on him for my inspiration, and the words pour out in perfect formation.

My Inner Plea

Heavenly Father please guide me; help me to be the best I can be. My desire is to do your will, it seems that my life is at a standstill. Help me to have a discerning mind; to shun evil of any kind. Help me to be an inspiration to someone else; that they may seek your righteousness, and forget about self. Please dear Lord! Help me to grow; show me the way you want me to go.

Troubled Mind

Lord I ask you to send me a healing; my mind is troubled, and I can't ignore this feeling. There is a conflict not fully reconciled; I thought I had made peace with it; I was fine for a while. Something about it just doesn't seem right; it's just left hanging, and not being brought to light. You know mind; you have already seen, Lord I ask you to please intervene; I know the answer was already there; you just waited on me to ask you in prayer.

The Greatest Gift

The greatest gift we have ever received, is Jesus Christ, for those who believe. There is no Christmas without Christ; the name itself shines his light. We were corrupt, and full of sin; that's when Jesus Christ stepped in. No one was worthy but the son; perfect in every way, he was the only one. He came wrapped in human flesh; the essence of God, to pay our debt. He was conceived in a supernatural way, and given to us on Christmas day.

When Love Abides

Love is the reason for the creation of man; the key to a better world, because united we stand. A God-given love from deep within, that lets us love everyone, no matter what color of their skin. When love abides for our fellow man, it will stop the murders that's plaguing the land. Love will cause a man to risk his life; to protect his friend, home, or wife. Love will stop all the universal greed, and cause us to someone in need. Love will stop the thief from breaking in, because all unrighteousness is sin. When love abides, our churches will come together as one; God does not separate, it was for all that he gave up his son. When love abides, we will live a christian life; the essence of love is; JESUS CHRIST.

The Last Word

When it's all said and done, God is the only one. He has the power to heal the sick; when he speaks, the problem is fixed. God allows doctors to do so much, but he is the one with the final touch. Whatever it is that's weighing you down, the peace of God will keep you sound. God controls all of our paths, he decides when we have walked our last. Be strong in all your burdens, and pray for peace of mind; stop worrying about your troubles; trust God to fix them in time. Be assured that God does hear; faith and trust will calm your fear. God has the last word when it's all said and done; he controls our lives and the final outcome.

What A Difference

What a difference a day makes; another chance to correct a mistake. Another day added to life; another day to fight a good fight. What a difference another day makes; to keep someone from making a big mistake. A day that transforms into night, to change what's wrong into right. What a difference another day makes; to encourage someone to be strong in their faith. We all have the hope of seeing another day; but it is not for us to say. What a difference another day makes; a day that God let us awake. A day that we are not promised to see, but by the grace of God, he let it be.

Unified

Real worship is focusing on God, his greatness, and his mercy. With a clean heart, God will not take a part; if we worship without a prepared heart. Pray for guidance day and night; God forgives when our heart is right. The church body must be unified, to offer true praise to the one who died. Come and forget the world outside; let the Spirit be your guide.

His Image

The human body is a well created machine; put together by the king of kings. Each intricate part was made with special care, fashioned by God himself, through a love he wanted to share. In his image, he made us great; but he already knew our fate. The temptation of satan was so great; it caused Adam and Eve to make a big mistake. He made us perfect in every way; until that one eventful day.

The Price Is Life

Through the sacrifice of God's only son, he wanted to do what had to be done; for this reason he did come. Our Lord and savior Jesus Christ; who willingly gave up his own life. He knew that he would suffer much, and that man would give him up. He knew that he would live again, by God the Father's mighty hand. So he paid the deadly price, for man to have eternal life.

In His Hands

All is quite and the night is still, as I lay down to sleep in God's holy will. I can feel his presence all around me at night; wrapped in his , and holding me tight; protecting me from the outside world; shielding me from danger and peril. Nothing can touch me if it's not in his plan; he controls all things by his command. All things are possible; and I'm able to stand; knowing there is safety in his powerful hands.

Blessed And Loved

As I stare at the sky above, and meditate on God's awesome love; my redeemer, and my strength; who forgives all sins to those who repent. He is waiting for you to let him in, before your redemption can begin. He wants us all to realize, that his love is the reason we are alive. He will return in the clouds one day, and wants us all to watch as well as pray.

A Marriage

Yes! I am married to Christ; he is my husband, I am his wife. He holds me tight in the still of the night; he let's me know everything will be alright. His love is beyond comprehension, it's felt in my heart with good intention. He is always with me wherever I go; he will never leave me, he told me so. I love him because he loved me first, he is the source of my rebirth. My husband Christ, will never lead me wrong; he will be there when others are gone. Yes! I am married to Christ; he is the best thing that ever happened in my life.

Sing Unto God Praises

What a friend we have in Jesus, our precious Lord who takes our hand; he will guide us over and help us to stand. The Lord will make a way; no matter what others may say. Just have a little with Jesus, and tell him all about your problems; because he lives. We can face our tomorrows. When your mind is weighed down, and you can't rest at night, God will rock you to sleep, until the morning light. He didn't bring us this far to leave us; his word is just and true; we are safe in his arms, no matter what we are going through. So hold on to God's unchanging hand; have a little faith, and believe that he can. Every praise is due or God; if we believe with our whole heart.

The Great I Am

I am the one who died on the cross; gave up my life, so your soul wouldn't be lost. I am the one that formed you from the dust of the ground. I am the one that open your eyes to a brand new day. I can heal any sickness with just one touch. I am the one who loves you so much. I am a comforter in times of grief. I will calm your mind with an inner peace. I am bread when you hunger; water when you thirst; as you travel through lide always keep me first. I am the one who can answer your prayer; just seek me first; I am always there. All things in creation is made by my hands, nothing was put here by the hands of man. I am all powerful, I am love, I am the Lord, your God above.

God's Handiwork

Thank you Lord for creating me; letting me be what only you can see. You know the thought of my heart, and every single body part. Every movement, every sensation; all limbs working through your creation. Man will budge the outside by what they see; only you know the inner me. I am unique in my own way, and have a gift that I display. We all have special gifts that God has endowed us with. We are all different in personalities and size, with skin of different shades; yet we are all the same in God's eyes. We are wonderfully made.

By And By

God watches over us while we slumber in sleep, resting in his perfect peace. So many things are happening all around, while we are resting safe and sound. Somewhere a child is being abused; men and women being falsely accused. Someone's all alone and have no food to eat; hiding in the shadows, living on the streets. We will never understand the things that God allow, the who, what, when, or how. All manner of things in this world taking place; yet we are still kept by his amazing grace.

Divided We Fall

Our hope should be for peace between all our sisters and brothers; to not let satan creep in and cause dissension against each other. There was a time when a man's word was his or her bond; now they are just words, which are meaningless to some. Selfish pride, and a need to be recognized, cause us to push others aside. Good will toward men are becoming a thing of the past; as Christians, our love for all people, should reach far and vast; because our hope is in Christ, the sustainer of all life. Our impact across this Nation, will mean nothing at all; if Christians are divided; then we fall.

God's Love

We all know what is required of us; that we love one another, and in God we trust. Why is it so hard for us to realize; we should look at the world through brand new eyes. As Christians, we should fully know, it takes real love in order to grow. We practice Sunday at the meeting love; not Agape love, which comes from above. Agape love will let us help one another; live everyday like there is no other. Love came down and died on the cross, to save a sinner like us, who once was lost.

My Deepest Thoughts

I know there is a better life waiting for me on the other side; yet doubt creeps in my thoughts I know I can't hide. I know you see inside my mind; Lord help me to let my light shine. Help me to live as a Christian each day, by letting you guide me in your own way. Help me to love you with all my heart and soul; help my praise to be genuine and bold. Help me to make a difference in someone's life; by telling them about your son Jesus Christ. Help me to love and do good toward all men, to not make a difference by the color of their skin. Help me to be strong, and just hold on; strengthen my faith, because I want to make Heaven my home.

The Living Lord

If you haven't accepted the Lord, just stop and think; your life could end before you even blink. No one knows the time or place, when the Lord will call them from this human race. Open you heart and mind; let his word sink in, the Lord will clean you up, and put away your sin. Step out on faith; leave the world outside; confess with your mouth, that Jesus Christ died; was crucified for the sins of men; buried, and then arose again; is alive today in the hearts of man. There can be no shame in accepting the Lord; only through belief will you gain your reward.

Life Is Short

Life is short, so don't waste your time; possessing things you will surely leave behind. Don't get wrapped up in this world of temptation, because worldly things can't give you salvation. Make each day count whenever you can; lend a helping hand to your fellow man. Encourage someone by letting them know; that God is there when they are burden down, and don't know where to go. Give thanks to God in your daily walk; by your actions, as well as your talk. Never put anyone else down; offer a smile, instead of a frown. Make each day count by letting God lead you, in all your decisions and he will carry you through. Life is short, and we just don't know; when it'll be our time to go.

All Inclusive

God is all inclusive in his love for man; no one is left out of his divine plan. He chose all of us, not just a few; there are no big I's or little you. He is all inclusive in the forgiveness of sins; which was covered by Jesus, when his life came to and end. He gave us the mind to choose the path we wanted to take in life; we will be judged by him, whether it's wrong or right. He is all inclusive in our daily need; he will order our steps, if we let him lead. He is all inclusive in his eternal prize; to walk the streets of heaven on the other side.

Prayer And Praise

I give you all the praise oh Lord, you created me and you know my every thought. You know the life I live; you know if my praise is real. I know I'm nothing on my own; only your mercy keeps me strong. I am comforted, because I know you are there; watching over me with your love and care. Thank you for the good and bad days, my faith in you is what pulls me through, and all my praise go up to you.

Be Thankful

God wants us to embrace life and enjoy it while we can, by living for him with love and compassion for every man. Be thankful for each day; for family and friends, and always pray. We should visit each other as often as we can; life is too precious to let slip through our hand. We think of all the things we could have done, at the sudden loss of a loved one. Time after time we wait to late, before we realize our mistake. Be thankful for the bad times as well as the good. Be thankful in all things as God said we should.

Give Me Strength

Oh Lord help me to hold on; build up my faith; help me to be strong. I know oh Lord, that soon one day; I will have to travel the very same way. I know that I'm on this earth for just a little while, and I will have to walk that last mile. Take away this fear that I feel inside; replace it with hope, and let peace abide.

Walking With Jesus

Lord I feel your presence all around; walking by my side, and keeping me sound. As I walk this road of life; you keep me on my feet; keep my legs from buckling underneath. When I feel like I'm sinking in a pool of quicksand; you grab my hand and pull me up again. You guide my steps, and keep me from harm. I know I am safe because of your arms.

A New Life

If people would only realize; in order to gain the eternal prize; we must live in a way,that pleases God everyday. Love and kindness are of God; it cannot live in an unclean heart. If there's a change in your heart and mind; the things of satan you leave behind. When we leave this earthly realm; we will all answer to him.

The Return

The Lord will come back for us one day, in all his glory, as the bible do say. Oh what a terrible time it will be, for those who didn't believe in the one who set them free. He will gather up all those who believed and trusted in him to hear their pleas. He has prepared for us a place; in a heavenly home where we will see God's face. No more worries about earthly things; only peace and happiness from the king of kings.

New Walk

I walk in the newness of life; because of love and a great sacrifice. Knowing that men are cruel and vain, but for our sake, Jesus was slain. The regeneration of my soul; he cleaned me up, and buried the old. With hope and faith, I hold on; knowing that God won't leave me alone. I walk in the newness of life; made possible through Jesus Christ.

Hold On

When your sunny days begin to grow dim, and the storms of life start to overwhelm, never give up hope because God is there, he knows your situation, and how much you can bare. Just believe that God will work everything out; trust in him and have no doubts. So hold on till your storms begin to clear, God will guide you and wipe away every tear.

A Secret Closet

The secret closet within my mind; lets me tune out the world, and leave it behind. I meditate on God when I am confused or sad; he restores the peace of mind that I once had. He picks me up when I've taken a fall; I meditate on God and he hears my call. He renews my strength when I'm weak and worn; and protects me from all hurt and harm.

Keep God First

God wants us to be happy in life, to keep him first and do what is right. Don't forget about him on our journey each day; because he is the one that is making our way. All that we own and everything we gain was made possible by God for us to attain. We didn't get to where we are today on our own; God has been there all along. He will keep us no matter where we are; he is with us near and far. So don't put God upon a shelf; and call on him when we have nothing left. Give thanks and praise at all times; when life is good or bad, and you will find, his peace restores your state of mind. Keep God first in your life, and all your battles he will fight. Lean on him and give him all praise; trust in him till the close of your days.

Help Me

Lord help me to edify your name, and not put your name to shame; help me to acknowledge you before all men, because you died for all of our sins. Help me to be strong and stand steadfast; not revert to things I did in the past. Give me the strength to resist temptation; while Satan is having his way in the nation. He knows that his time is not long, and is doing all he can to steer men wrong. Help me to humble myself before you; I know without you, there's nothing I can do. Help me to let your light shine through me from above; Help me to live a life of goodwill and love.

The Spirit

I'm not one that talks very much, but the spirit of God has a special touch. It fills me with peace within my soul; gives me the courage to be bold. I know it's nothing but the spirit of God that makes me shout out when he moves upon my heart. There is a calmness of body and mind, a state of being that's so divine. The presence of God keeps me sound, when chaos is happening all around. I don't worry or have a care, when the peace of God is resting there.

My Way Or No Way

Human beings are creatures of habit; they do things in a certain way and will not vary no matter what anyone say. To do things different would be wrong, and the ideals they value would be gone. It's hard for some to accept change, so they would rather do things the same. I know there are some things people do, and some places they go; are completely wrong if I may say so. Change is good if done with a right mind; it protects what you value at the same time. Just because it's different, doesn't make it wrong; my way or no way is just the same old song.

A Good Heart

The heart of a Christian is humble and kind; with no thoughts of malice in their mind. A good heart will help you if they can; by offering you a helping hand. They will not run all over town, and spread what they did for you all around. A good heart is patient, and don't mind waiting; don't mind giving instead of taking. A good heart does not cause confusion and fights; they reason together, to set things right. A good-hearted Christian is trying to live for God; but Satan put up roadblocks to try and make it hard. A good-hearted Christian will stand their ground; and call on God to make Satan back down. A good-hearted Christian that's dedicated to Christ; will not give up, and fight the good fight.

One People, One Purpose

God made us different, so we wouldn't all be the same. That doesn't mean that one race has more privilege to call upon his name. He made us flesh and bone covered by a variety of skin tones. He scattered us all over the world; confused the language of man, woman, boy and girl. He made us all to praise and worship him; to be a witness to others of his heavenly realm. We are all different; yet our purpose for being here is the same, to lift up Jesus before men and praise to his mighty name.

Women Of Age

You wear it well, your grace of age; a strong woman whom God has made. You've made it through so much down through the years; by faith, hard work and many tears. God has brought you all the way; He has never left you, and is with you today. So just hold on and keep running this race of life; till the end of your journey when there will be no more pain and strife. Women of age who are graceful and wise; women of God who will inherit the eternal prize. Women of age, be proud of who you are; for you are God's shining star.

The Rainbow

The rainbow in the sky is a promise from God; who cannot lie. The earth would not be destroyed by another flood; another covenant was made through Jesus' blood. He reminds himself with the rainbow; and set it in the sky for all his children to know. If you look up at the sky after the storm; you will see the rainbow beginning to form. A promise of God to all mankind; the beautiful rainbow he sends as a sign.

No Explanation

I can't explain the love of God; but it extends from heart to heart. His love is beyond our comprehension; to give up His son with deliberate intention. God created us out of love; he protects, and we are to serve. I can't explain the love of God; but it is felt within my heart. He said he would never leave us; we just have to believe and trust. Bad things happen we can't understand. No one can explain it; it's all in God's hands.

My Creation

I am knocking at the door of your heart. I am your Creator and Father God. Open your eyes that you may see; everything in the Universe exists by me. Clear your mind and meditate on me; complete submission is the key. Let the depth of my love penetrate your mind, and know the reason I died for mankind. Open your ears that you may hear; my word of salvation loud and clear. Pray for understanding and how to discern; read my word and you will learn. Children of mine don't shut me out; believe in me and have no doubt. Believe in me that I am He ; who turned water into wine, and parted the Red Sea. Children of my creation since time began; I have watched over you with a mighty hand. Children of mine let my spirit flow; so that where I am you will also go. Trust in me and let me guide; I will walk with you and never leave your side.

What A Friend

True friends influence those with whom they associate, to rise a little higher, and be a little better. We as a people in the natural state, need a friend to whom we can relate. Someone that won't spread your business all over town, or kick you when you are already down. Someone close you can confide in; that has your back until the end. As you live and share the gospel of Jesus Christ, you will attract people to you who will want to be in your life. We also must strive to be a friend to others, and let our light shine forth. Our influence will bless the lives of many; but oh, what a supernatural friend we have in Christ, who will guide us through the troubles of this life. All your secrets are safe in His arms, and if you stumble, he will protect you from harm. What a mighty friend on whom we can call; Jesus Christ, a friend to all.

What He Is To Me

What is God to me? He is love, He is peace, all power is in his hand; he is everlasting to everlasting, stretched out all over this land. Without him, I would not be, he gave me this life of mine; truly is he the one divine. I could not move a muscle if it wasn't for him, only he controls my body and limbs. With him in my life, I am able to bare the pain and strife. It is only through him that I open my eyes, to each new day, whatever may arise.

The Ultimate Price

Easter represents the risen Christ, who died and rose so that we could have eternal life. The most precious gift that God had to give; was given to us, so that we could live. He came to earth to pay a sin debt, but he had to die before we could collect. He was whipped, mocked, and crucified; hung on a cross until he died. Abandoned by the disciples he led, they were afraid, so they fled; they did not fully understand; what he meant when he said he would rise again. He is alive and glorified; sitting in heaven on his father's right side. All of our sins have been forgiven; because the ultimate price has already been paid.

God's Checklist

Are you living the life I require of you? Are you giving me thanks for all that I've done, and will do? Are you studying my holy word? To know for yourself, instead of what you've heard. Are you doing all you can to lift up my name? Because to live for me, there can be no shame. Do you give me praise wherever you go? Are you letting your light shine, so an unsaved world can know. If others can see my light in you; it will cause them to want to know me too. You are a testament to a world full of sin; others need to know that on me they can depend.

Come Back To Reality

There are some that think they will never die; to them the word just doesn't apply. I know, because of the way I used to be; the mindset I had was that death couldn't touch me. We delude ourselves in the worst possible way, by assuming we are here to stay. I gave my heart to God, my sins he did forgive, he opened up my understanding, and taught me how to live. When we accept this life on earth won't last; only then can we appreciate what must come to pass. I don't care who you are; rich, poor, near, or far; what we must ultimately realize, there is no place we can run or hide. God sees and knows all, he is in control, and we will answer his call. This is the only way we can get to the other side, to cross over by death, and with Jesus abide.

Unholy Union

God made man for woman, and woman for man; no same sex union is in his plan. When you let satan take control your mind; you think what you are doing is perfectly fine. Parents, I know you love your children, but do not support them in that lifestyle; you're saying it's okay if they live that way; instead of telling them what the word of God say. Men have just hardened their heart, living their own way. God left it up to man to make the laws of this land; the passing of this law is by satan's hand.

The Plan Of Salvation

God so loved the world; he gave his only begotten son. God the father, and God the son, in agreement they are one. Born of a Hebrew virgin girl; Jesus Christ entered the world. Son of God, clothed in human flesh, was given the strength to face the ultimate test. He was delivered by Judas into the enemy's hand, all according to God's plan. Believe in the name of the Lord Jesus Christ; he suffered and died that we may have life. Jesus Christ the son of man; God raised him up with all power in his hand. Jesus Christ the son of man; ascended back to Heaven, but is coming again.

The Hope You Carry

When people wound you with stinging words, and some just with their eyes; before you retreat inside yourself, just always realize; it matters not the things they say, or how they make you feel; the hope you carry in your heart is what they'll never steal. They'll take away the sun from your blue sky, but not the peace inside; they'll see discomfort on your face, but not the hurt you hide. You'll have distress for one dark night while tender scars are forming, but you have God's promise from his word, "joy comes in the morning". Just hold fast to your white robe till the sun breaks through at last, and praise God that he's helped you weather one more stormy blast.

I Exist

Lord I thank you for my life, my very existence, through your pain and strife. I know no matter what I go through; I have to lean and depend on you. You can do all things and never fail; unlike men, who are weak and frail. You provide my spiritual feed, maintain my body with all I need. You raise me up when I am down; put a smile on my face, instead of a frown. I know that things will be alright; peace is restored, my heart is light. I only exist because of you; because of you I can make it through.

Make A Choice

Whose side are you on? The side of right, or the side of wrong. Will you be able to stand the test? To live for God in a world of unrest. Will you give in to satan's snares? or hold on to God in constant prayers. Will you follow those you know are doing wrong? Then expect rewards when you get to your heavenly home. Who are you trying to please, your so called friends, by following their lead. Whose side are you on? God will be there when your friends are gone. Ask yourself these questions, then stand your ground; or will you let pride and greed take you down. Whose side are you on? The time is now, there are no do overs when you take your last bow.

Gave Up To Raise Up

God looked down on sinful man, that he made from the dust by his mighty hand. The people committed a great sin against God; he regretted he made them, and hardened his heart. Made to serve and worship him, but for sin they were condemned. He was ready to destroy them all, but Jesus stepped in to take the fall. No one was worthy in the land, so Jesus said "I'll go down and redeem man". Prepared from the time of his birth, Jesus Christ came down to earth. God sent his only son, to be sacrificed for everyone. God gave him up, in order to raise him up. We would all be lost, if Jesus had not paid the cost.

A New Creature

When God truly change your heart, he gives you a new beginning, a new start. You are a new person, saved by God's grace; his light in you will show upon your face. The world to you will not look the same; everything is fresh and new, through the eyes of salvation, God has given you. The desire to do the things you did before, become unimportant to you anymore. Don't let satan cause your light to grow dim, by giving in to his every whim. He'll speak to your mind, and control your thoughts; make you forget the word of God you've been taught. It is his job to get you to stray, don't be deceived by what he may say. You are a new creature, endowed with God's light; embrace your salvation, and let it shine bright.

Read Your Bible

Everything happening in this world has been foretold; read your bible as to how it unfold. The time is now to turn to God for your soul salvation. Times will get hard, only God can supply our needs, in a world full of turmoil, deceit, and greed. The love of many will wax cold; thieves and murderers are becoming bold. Men are lovers of themselves, with hardened hearts, and no love for anyone else. False prophets and teachers are on the rise, using God as their disguise. Earthquakes, floods, a rebellious generation, uncommon weather all across the nation. Wars being fought in other lands; we should not worry, because God will help us stand. The bible tells us these things must come to pass. Read your bible, and pray without ceasing; seek wisdom and knowledge for your increasing. Read your bible and trust God's word; I am just a messenger trying to be heard.

God's Majesty

I stare up at the clear blue sky, so vast and wide to the naked eye. A white puff of clouds slowly appear, it seems I could touch them, they are so near. If I look at them long enough; I can see the movement of the white cloud puff. It changes its shape as it move along; then slowly disappears and it is gone. The great clear blue encompass all around; from the dome shaped top down to the ground. As I stare into the great clearblue, it seems to draw even closer to you, it wraps you like a blanket that's warm and secure; soft as cotton, and oh so pure. So majestic, and so wide, under God's creation we all abide. The great clearblue is so vast and deep; no matter how far you go up, it can't be reached. God's majesty is at work, as we walk this life upon the earth.

Be Real

If men would live the life they profess; our lives would be much more blessed. We often pass each other on the street; some of us don't even speak. We say that we are God's child, it's not costing us to smile. We use profane language in order to fit in; around worldly people we call our friends. Instead of conforming to their ways; we should be telling them how they can be saved. Our conduct plays a vital part, if the love of God is in our heart. Be real in your service to God, because he knows all mens hearts...

Show Yourself Approved

My experience with Christian people let's me know; much of their righteousness is based on show. We say we have forgiven, but do we really? We say we love, but do we sincerely? If we are holding something in our heart, let it go; I know it's hard, but give it to God. If you let it fester for to long; it will spread like cancer your bone. I am a Christian myself. I am always asking God to forgive me, and create in me a clean heart. Our hearts have to be right; God don't play, he sees our pretense each and every day.

Tempted

Satan is a trickster, he'll try and cloud your mind; he's the author of confusion; he knows that he has a short time. He'll try to pull you away from God by putting temptation in your path; he'll show you worldly things, that you always wished you had. He'll whisper things into your ear and say "there's nothing wrong with that" until his thoughts become yours; then you begin to react. When he has gained control of your mind, to the things of God you have become blind. If you succumb to his enticement, he will have accomplished his goal; to turn you away from God, to try and claim your soul.

Be Careful

Be careful in your daily walk; stop and think before you talk. We are not in this world alone; when we mistreat others, we will atone. Stop and think before you act; you just might say something you can't take back. Be careful thinking you are above everyone else, because your righteousness is focused on self. Be careful in all you seek to achieve; there is no gain if you try to deceive. Life is too short for confusion and fights, instead of just treating each other right. Be careful not to criticize; we all fall short in God's eyes.

The Trouble With Christians

The trouble with Christians in the world today, are material things that lead them astray. The way of God we have left behind, and selfish pride have clogged our minds. We should thank God each and every day, and not be concerned with things that will pass away. All that we have, and are able to do, is by the grace of God who watches over you.

Jesus Lives

Jesus died to save us all, young; old; big; and small. Crucified upon the cross, he died for sinners that were lost. God so loved the world, that's the reason why, Jesus came to earth, and was prepared to die. God does not discriminate, he loves all the human race. Jesus arose on easter day, and overcame death in a powerful way.

Belief Is The Key

Our lives should reflect our commitment to God; through compassion for others, and a loving heart. Some people live their lives on their own terms; they say when you are dead you are done. They continue to live their lifestyle of sin, and have chosen not to let God in. Belief is the key that unlocks the door to your heart, you have the choice to open it or not. Don't fool yourself into thinking you will get away. Everything you do, you will have to answer for one day. God knows your heart, and the thoughts inside, because from him, you just can't hide.

Exaltation

Oh Lord I see your beautiful universe, and meditate on your awesome power. I feel your magnificence in this very hour. As I look up toward heaven, I see your greatness in the clouds rolling by. I see clusters of white clouds sailing across a clear blue sky; when just moments ago, dark stormy clouds hovered on high. Only on you can I depend; when the storms of life start creeping in. Oh Lord, I praise your holy name; through whom all power forever reigns.

When Tomorrow Comes

When tomorrow comes, I'll give my life to Christ; leave the past behind, and begin a new life. When tomorrow comes. When tomorrow comes, I'll drop a line; try to make up for so much lost time. When tomorrow comes. When tomorrow comes I'll apologize, for all the secrets and all the lies. When tomorrow comes. When tomorrow comes, I'll do a good deed, help someone that's really in need. When tomorrow comes. When tomorrow comes, I'll show more love; as God commands from up above. When tomorrow comes, I'll do this or that we say; putting off for tomorrow what we can do today. We take for granted that our tomorrows will always be; when tomorrow comes is not promised to you or me.

There Is A purpose

Everything in nature is here for a reason; only God knows the purpose of each season. The picturesque leaves on all the trees; with many different colors that sway in the breeze. The pure white snow that fall to the ground; blankets the earth without a sound. Sleet, ice, wind, and rain; oh let us give praise to God's holy name. The beauty of nature is a magnificent sight, by the creator of all things; through his glory and might.

Look Around You

Look out at the world around you and see; without a God, none of this would be. The miracle of nature; everything in sight; sun, moon, day, and night. God's infinite power and love is beyond comprehension, he speaks to the wind, and it pays attention. Spoke a word and bones came together; calmed the raging sea in perilous weather. Fed a multitude of people with five loaves of bread; healed the sick, and brought back the dead. Blew the breath of life into dust from the ground; covered it with flesh from foot to crown. In his own image he created mankind; schulpeded him with love according to his perfect design. Look out at the world around you and see, without a God, where would we be.

Ever Present

When it seems like nothing has gone right; God is there to take up your fight. He is there waiting on you, to ask him for your breakthrough. Prayer is the key that will keep us strong, it opens the door, and helps us hold on. God will guide our thought process, and let us be able to stand the test. He is ever present, and knows what we need; let him take the wheel, and he will lead.

Welcome: Celebration

We celebrate Easter because you see, Jesus came to save both you and me. We celebrate Easter because our Lord, died and arose on our accord.

Easter

Jesus died on Calvary, and rose again for you and me. Harken to the words I've said, Jesus is alive, he is not dead.

Merciful Father

Merciful is our Father above; be thankful for his never ending love. He gave His life for me and you; something He did not have to do. Peace of mind he gives to us; if only in Him we put our trust. Merciful is our father on high; he knows your heart, and he hears your cry. Grace has saved us all today; through faith He'll take us all the way.

Christ And The Single Life

Although you can not see it now, just believe that God will send you your soulmate. Trust in him and patiently wait. To live single in God is to sacrifice; to resist the temptations that come in life. Ask God to take it away from you; lean on Him and he will bring you through. If you try to find someone on your own; you'll choose someone completely wrong. What God has meant for you will always be there; He move in his own time; you just continue in prayer. According to His will it will be done; when God sends you that certain someone.

The Lamb

We were sent a Savior on Christmas day; to offer redemption, and show us the way. Born through a lowly virgin girl; the way God chose Him to enter the world. At the age of twelve his mission began; to preach salvation throughout the land. He knew the things He had to endure, but our salvation He wanted to ensure. On this day our Savior was born; was mocked by man, and brought to scorn. He lived among men, but did not sin; was tempted by Satan, but didn't give in. The Bible tell of his wonderful story; to our Lord and Savior be all the glory.

I Learned To Lean

A house can be a scary, lonely place when you are left all alone, but I call on the Lord to keep me strong. In a world full of sin today; I've learned how to lean, and he takes my fear away. I used to jump at every bump, and cringe at every high wind; thinking a tornado was coming, or someone was trying to break in. I have no weapons to protect myself; I've learned how to lean on Jesus and no one else. I'm secure in the knowledge that the Lord is watching over me; and that whatever is his will, it will be.

Lord I

I tried to live life on my own, all the while, I knew it was wrong. You gave me free will to make a choice, I did not heed my inner voice. I thought only of satisfying my human needs, because of that, I succumbed to greed. I made a decision to commit a sin, my conscious condemned me, and guilt spread within. I know you see everything I do, I should have stood still and waited on you. No excuse can make right, it's an abomination in your sight. I come to you with a sincere plea, please Heavenly Father, please forgive me. Give me the strength to be strong; to resist the temptation to do wrong.

Someone Cares

Sometimes it may feel like no one cares, just look to the Lord who's always there. Just believe that the Lord will take care of you, and that he will see you through. All your burdens will be easier to bare, when hope and faith replace your despair.

Welcome

To the pastor, pulpit guest, members, and visiting friends. Welcome to the house of the Lord; let us praise him on one accord. I stand before you now to let you know; Jesus welcomed us over two thousand years ago. Let the spirit guide you on this day; you are welcome to sing, shout, talk,or pray.

Reconciliation

God knew that man would sin, he is Alpha and Omega, the beginning and the end. He already had a master plan; a divine sacrifice to redeem man. We were reconciled through his son Jesus Christ; by the shedding of his blood, he gave up his life. Jesus died for the sins of all men, it's by his blood, through faith in him that God forgives our sins.

Limited Power

I will always depend on you Lord, no matter how bad my situation get, my determination is strong, and my mind is set. I will trust in you with no regret. I know that whatever I go through; satan will try and get me to turn on you. You are the potter, and he is the clay; he can do no more than what you say. There is a limit that you let him reach; beyond that, his power will cease. All things are possible for you to do; satan is just no match for you.

Remember Me

We often sing the hymn 'Lord remember me", but have we forgotten about him, and how he set us free. Do we remember the promise we made if he forgave us for our sins; to live our life for him, and praise him before all men. Do we remember to thank him for bringing us out of life's storms, because only through him are we truly reborn. Do we remember to thank him before the setting of the sun each day; because he is the potter, and we are the clay. Do we remember to thank him for all his love and care; for guiding us through this life, and for always being there. The very essence of life is given to everyone; without him, nothing can be done. Just remember there is power in his name; he will be with us always, and that will never change.

When The Lord Came

When the Lord came, he brought salvation; when the Lord came, he died for all nations. When the Lord came and saved my soul; I became refined as pure gold. When the Lord came, everything looked new; the light of my savior was shining through. Same old body, but peace of mind, he's always with me in good or bad times. When the Lord came, I was able to lay all my burdens down; told him my problems, he didn't spread them around. When the Lord came, he washed all my sins away; he gave me hope and faith, in looking toward a brighter day.

God Is My Doctor

Just after dark one evening at home; me and my two children were there alone. I fed the children, and put them to bed; after a while I got a pain in my head, soon after that I got a terrible backache, I had never felt pain so great. I decided to just go to bed, with pain shooting through my back and head. It felt like my body was being crushed in a vice; and every move I made did not suffice. The children were to young to send out for help, and there were no other options left. I prayed to the Lord to take the pain away, and help me get some rest. I put myself in his hands, and laid upon his breast. I drifted off to sleep in pain, calling on my Jesus name; then about the midnight hour, God spoke to my mind with mighty power, "wake up, your apartment was torn down, but now it's built up again" he said it in a language he knew I would understand. (At that time, I lived in an apartment building). My eyes opened wide; I got up and moved around, all my pain was gone, from my back to my crown. I gave thanks to the lord, for healing my body from this great discord. I checked on the children, got a drink of water, and went back to bed. I thanked the Lord again for doing what he said. He is my doctor.

A Way Out Of No Way

I was in the wrong place at the wrong time; caught in a situation that keeps coming back to mind. I was looking down the barrel of a gun pointed straight at my head; I would not do what this person had said, I thought that I would wind up dead. I prayed to the Lord in my mind, "please God, help me get out of this bind". The Lord intervened, and caused a natural act; the person with the gun had to step back. The Lord made a way for me to get out of a situation I could do nothing about. God took control and made my path clear; he regulated my mind, and calmed all my fear.

Be Still

Be still and let God work; life is full of disappointments and hurt. There are some things we just can't fix. We can try as hard as we can, but it may not be in God's plan. If we stop trying to do things on our own, and just be still and let it alone. God knows what's best for us, so just be still and learn to trust.

A Change Of Face

We change faces like we change clothes; we wear them awhile just to fit the role. Our around the house face becomes a whole different case, when we change into that every day pace. We shun the sinner man, and don't even speak; whenever we pass them on the street. We slip into something more comfortable, like our better than others face; pass by our christian brothers and sisters like we don't have the time to waste; pretend you didn't see them, because you were in such a haste. We put on our Sunday at the meeting face, with lots of smiles and gentle embrace. The faces we had on all week long, we should know that they were wrong. We change our face like we change our clothes; slip on this, put on that, try on those. A face for each day of the week; only God knows what's truly underneath.

Just A Blessing

We take for granted each beautiful day: get up in the morning and don't even think to say, thank you Lord, for another blessed day. We never give a thought to how precious each day is; yet another chance God gives us to live. Each day he gives us can make a difference in someone's life; can cause them to seek Jesus, and his wonderful light. Another blessed day to lend a listening ear, or give an encouraging word to calm one's fear. Just another blessing that the Lord in his mercy gives, each and everyday that he allows us to live.

Reflection

Heavenly father, when I read or hear about the illness and misfortune of others; I realize that I am truly blessed compared to my other sisters and brothers. Father I pray for a healing of all those in pain; I ask this in your son Jesus mighty name.

A Mighty God

All things are possible through God who strengthens you; there is nothing too hard for him to do. Problems will come without a doubt, he is the one that can work them out. He will make a way when there is none; when all seems hopeless, and there's nowhere to turn. Hold on to his hand, don't let go;he will raise you up when you sink to low. God is majestic in his mighty power; he watches over creation from his heavenly tower. The warmth of his love will bring you in from the cold; he will calm your mind, and restore peace to your soul.

Christmas

Christmas comes but once a year; we exchange gifts with holiday cheer. The true meaning of the Christmas season, should give us joy for only one reason. God gave to us on Christmas day; his only son Jesus, to light our way. Christmas is a time to reflect upon Christ, a time for love and a celebration of life. God's love is so great, it should fill our hearts; where we would want to follow Jesus, and never depart.

Mama And The Preacher

Mama raised me up in the right way; taught me the value of life, and to never forget to pray. She took me to church on sunday morning, to learn of Jesus and how he was born. I had to sit and listen to the preacher preach; I couldn't laugh, move, or speak. My mother taught me to treat everybody right, to show love, and kindness, because this was good in God's sight. I didn't realize it at the time; that the words of the preacher would stick in in my mind. I believe in the word of God's divine plan; the sacrifice of his son for the salvation of man. The way mama raised me when I was growing up; impacted my life so very, very much.

Material Gain

We should be content with the necessities of life, all this material gain will only cause strife. I often feel material things just get in the way; there's enough stress with all the bills we have to pay. All the things we don't really need, are simply do to our personal greed. I look around at the things in my house; most of them I can do without. Do you ever get tired of the material gain; after all, it's only vain. These things you will leave behind when you leave this world; to be fought over, given away, or put up for sell.

Ancestors

Our ancestors in earlier years, were oppressed and brought to tears. they were robbed of the right to be their own man; were bought and sold as house and field hands; even in all their oppression and grief; their faith was strong, and it gave them relief. There were many blacks down through history, that fought for the right just to be free, to be treated as equal, with pride and dignity. Freedom of choice like any other man, for this they were willing to take a stand. They prayed and sang hymns to overcome someday, and leaned on the Lord to guide their way. Our ancestors, through blood, sweat, and tears; made it possible for us down through the years. They fought for the freedom we have today, to live, and speak in our own way.

Time Don't Wait

Hours, days, and weeks go past; then we say "time sure went fast". Just in the course of a normal day; before you know it, time has slipped away. The time we lose can never be gotten back, when it comes to time; we can't afford to be slack. What we can't seem to realize, is that time don't wait on us to rise. If there's anything you want to do; see, or help someone less fortunate than you; make the most of the time you have, instead of letting it go to waste; time don't wait, so tread carefully, but make haste. Time is precious, and shouldn't be lost, because sooner or later, we'll pay the cost.

Season Of Joy

We are blessed today, just to be here; God looked down on us with favor to see this time of year. We come together once again, in the season God gave us the redeemer of man. A God who loves us in spite of our weaknesses and flaws; he came into the world for this very cause. His love for us is like no other; unconditional, by his blood we are covered. We give praise to him, and lift up his name, with fellowship and love, with all minds the same. Let Christ be the focus of one mind; with all our praise together combined.

Divine Experience

Friday, October Twenty Third, Nineteen Eighty Seven; I experienced what seemed like my death. I wasn't sick or in bad health that I knew of; it could have been a dream, but oh so real it seemed. I was wide awake, and getting out of bed; all of a sudden a dizzy feeling swept over my head. I stood up, and became very unstable; I tried to steady myself, but I wasn't able. All at once, I fell straight back; I didn't have enough time to fully react. When my body hit the bed, I thought that I would soon be dead. I was semi- conscious and yet aware, of what was happening to me as I lay there. All of a sudden I was over the bed; looking down at myself, when I heard a voice that said "come on home in the name of the Lord" I just lay there numb and still; thinking no, not now, I'm not ready to die, but if it's your will. There was no pain, no fear, only peace; then I said "thank you Lord" and everything around me seemed to cease. At that moment I felt a rush of air fill my nose; God restored my life and soul, he opened my eyes, and made me whole.

Without Jesus

Without Jesus, where would we be? We could do nothing; you or me. Without Jesus, we would have no hope; in fear and darkness, we would grope. If Jesus had not died for us, in who else would we put our trust? If Jesus had not risen from the grave; how else could our souls be saved? Without Jesus coming to earth; we would not have a new birth.

A Private Place

There's a special place I go, when I'm feeling down and low. A place I go to be alone; a private place right in my home. It's a special room to me; a place that's comforting to be. Once I go in and shut the door; nothing around me exist anymore. Do you have a private place? A place to go just in case.

By His Word

The earth was dark, had no form, and water was everywhere, but by the divine power of God, who was already there; he spoke a word, and gave order and form to the universe. He separated dark from light, and called it day and night. The waters from the earth; the land from the sea; to make it habitable for you and me. He spoke a word and the earth obeyed his command; to bring forth vegetation for humans and animals that would populate the land. He declared "it was good".

I Cry Alone

Why do I cry alone when there is grief; instead of sharing my pain to gain relief? Why do I cry alone, and not let the tears out; isn't that what grief is all about? I can't help but feel the pain, when others' tears pour down like rain. Why is it my tears won't flow, when I'm at my lowest low? I try to be strong, and just hold on, but everything changes when I get home; I find myself crying alone. All the memories flood my head; of all the things that people said. Why Lord, do I cry alone; why not let my emotions be shown?

The Color Of Lies

White or black, a lie is a lie; it makes no difference the reason why. A lie of a different color, is still a lie my sister or brother. What is a little white lie anyway; the telling of it does not make it okay. The big black lie can cause destruction, and lead to all other types of corruption. Some lies we tell may hurt ourselves, but it's a problem when they hurt someone else. You can paint a lie any color you want; red, green, white, black, or blue; sooner or later, that lie will catch up with you.